Divine
Whispers...

Melissa Giomi

Melissa Giomi
Facebook: @MelissaGiomiauthor
Instagram: @melissa.giomi

First Paperback Edition September 2024

The Living Bible copyright ©1971 by Tyndale House Foundation. Used by permission of Tyndale House Publishers Inc., Carol Stream, Illinois 60188. All rights reserved. The Living Bible, TLB, and the The Living Bible logo are registered trademarks of Tyndale House Publishers. THE HOLY BIBLE, NEW INTERNATIONAL VERSION®, NIV® Copyright ©1973, 1978, 1984, 2011 by Biblica, Inc.® Used by permission. All rights reserved worldwide.

ISBN 979-8-218-43737-4 (paperback)
ISBN 979-8-218-43738-1 (ebook)

Library of Congress Control Number: 2024913762

Edited by Pia Edberg, piaedberg.com
Blurb by Book Blurb Magic, IG: @bookblurbmagic
Cover & interior design by Karolina Wudniak, karolinawudniak.com

ALSO BY MELISSA GIOMI:

Divine Encounters…

Divine Appointments…

Table of Contents

Holy Ground

Peace

Presence

Introduction

I'm delighted you have picked up *Divine Whispers...* This is my third book joining *Divine Encounters...* and *Divine Appointments...* on their journey into the world.

I am grateful these books give me the opportunity to share the healing, peace, and joy I have experienced as I walk with Jesus.

This journey continues to be full of thrilling, peaceful, joy-filled moments mixed with sadness, fear, and the unknown. Lessons learned through a long battle with breast cancer taught me that there is always hope.

My prayer is that while you journey with me through Divine Whispers..., you will discover that the Divine is all around you, as close as your next breath. I pray you will feel His whispers brush your skin and hear them dance in the breeze. May He reveal His peace and presence in an ordinary day and His joy and healing in the ancient rhythms of nature.

I hope you find exactly what you need in the pages of this book and are richly blessed. Peace be with you. Thank you for reading my book.

Acknowledgments

Divine Whispers... came to be as God whispered His words and ideas from His heart to my pen.

There are many that need a shout-out for helping me launch this book.

To...

My family—my husband, Paul, and our adult children, Emma and Josh; my parents, Mike and Nancy; my sister and brother-in-law, Nicole and Tim—for believing in me, reading my books and praying.

Wendy Moon, Tina Harrell, and Jen Cole for the blessings of long-lasting friendship, and your prayers, encouragement, and feedback in all things as Divine Whispers... came to be.

Heather Greaves, Jainell Gaitan, and Kathryn Dunn thank you for your treasured friendship and invaluable feedback on wording and design ideas, as well as your fresh eyes and thoughtful suggestions.

My military mamas! Archna, Kellie, Stephanie, Sherri, Megan, April, Tracy, Ann, Andrea, Ana, Tina, Julie, Mary, Maria, Ruth and Alyssa. You all are a blessing with your encouragement, shared tears, humor, and embracing the suck in this crazy season of life. You are brave, courageous women that I'm honored to call my dear friends.

The talented women who transform my rough drafts into books I am proud to send into the world. Pia Edberg for editing and sharpening up my words and thoughts so the voice of my book is heard, Jessie Cunniffe for bringing those words together into a beautiful blurb that draws you in, and Karolina Wudniak for interior formatting and creating cover designs that perfectly capture the soul and essence of my books.

You are all appreciated!

His Breath...

His Breath is a whisper,

His Song is a sigh.

He dances in the wind,

The Creator is nigh.

Holy Ground

Hallowed

THE WORD HALLOWED often evokes a mysterious and magical feeling. Supernatural. Visions of sacred, lovely light and silence swirl in my mind—a sense of something in the atmosphere crackling with divine prophesy. Holy ground—a place where angels and heavenly beings tread.

In my limited understanding of all things Divine, these images come from the knowledge that a place deemed hallowed has been consecrated and made holy by the divine presence of God.

Imagine a quiet neighborhood in the early morning hours, still sleepy from a night of peaceful rest. A man and his dog venture out for their morning constitutional. The beauty of the morning, the sleepy quiet of the houses, and the cool air on his skin bring a smile to his face and a lightness to his steps. Heavy things are weighing on him. This lovely morning soothes his spirit and invites conversation with the Creator. As he spills his fears and concerns to the Father, he is enveloped in such peace;

peace that shouldn't be here in light of his circumstances and worries, yet it is. The Father soothes and speaks provision and safety into his tired soul. Hallowed.

The woman on her bike follows the paved path through the city on her way to work. The busy street, impatient drivers, and slow-moving pedestrians blur as she frets over the presentation she will be giving in a few hours. Is she prepared? Did she remember to hit all the important points? Will what she says make sense? Her mind spins and panic tries to surface, so she lifts up a quick prayer asking for wisdom and courage. As she pedals, her thoughts come together more clearly. She remembers the hard work she put into this presentation and the success she's had in the past. She is enough and deeply loved. Her worries dim and fade. Excitement replaces fear as her tense shoulders and churning insides relax. The Lord is with her; she can do this. Hallowed.

Night falls in the campground as the older couple settles into their camp chairs to relax and unwind before bed. The campfire dances and sparks, giving off a warm, happy glow as s'mores fixings are passed between them. The peace of the Redwoods falls around them, filling them with a sense of belonging. They find peace in nature. Listening to the forest slow down for the night, the feeling of being wrapped up and carefully tended to fill their souls. They know they are in the presence of the Holy One. Their campground in the Redwoods is hallowed ground. The Creator is everywhere. He whispers peace in the wind sighing through the trees, and sings provision as His creatures scout for food in the nooks and crannies of the forest floor. He speaks joy into this season of life as the campfire snaps and cracks. Hallowed ground.

Wherever life takes you today, myriad opportunities are waiting to usher you into the presence of the Divine. He is everywhere. Divine encounters and Divine appointments are waiting like hidden treasures to be found. Where the Spirit of the Lord is, there is peace, healing, hope, and freedom. Hallowed ground.

Promises

BREE'S FAVORITE TRAIL isn't far from home. She can drive there in about fifteen minutes, give or take, if you factor in the morning traffic. The aroma of her medium latte macchiato swirls through the truck as it warms her hands at the stoplight. The sunbeams hitting the prism hanging from her rearview mirror shatter and regroup into lovely rainbows and shimmery light. The way the colors land on the dashboard and the sleeve of her hoodie bring a soothing feeling of hope and promises whispered and kept.

The parking lot at the trailhead is partially full. Perhaps she will find the clarity and peace she's seeking without the distraction of other trail-walkers. Freedom to clearly hear the confirmation she's looking for is uppermost in her mind. There are too many voices with strong opinions, sage advice, and "words from the Lord" coming at her from all sides. Everyone has an opinion and the chaos of them all is deafening.

Bree knows this trail with its curves, slight hills, and beautiful trees offering shade and bright patches of warm sunlight. It's her go-to place when the chaos becomes suffocating and her tired mind needs a break. It is important that she re-focus on Jesus and what He promised.

Nature is the sacred sanctuary where she finds Him. His breath is in the breeze, and His laughter in the birdsong and busy chatter of animals that call the forest home. His love dances in the patches of sunlight that gently warm her skin and His peace, that glorious peace. It enfolds her with the scents of pine, warm soil, ancient things, and nature. Holy. Sacred.

Moving further along the trail, Bree hears that lovely silence, the gift of the forest. Her mind begins to slough off the voices and the "shoulds." The contrasting coolness of the woodsy air and the warmth of the sun penetrating the open spots of the canopy feel brisk and invigorating. Peeling off the hoodie, she picks up the pace, savoring the competing chill and warmth of the trail. As she ties the hoodie around her waist, she notices the tattoos on her arms. *Be Still* and *Faith Over Fear*. In her busyness, she's forgotten the deeply personal meaning of these words inked into her skin. They are reminders of life-changing circumstances and words she heard Him speak over her—prophesy and promises. Promises…

Quieting her mind, she finds a spot off the path to sit and wait to hear from Him. She has questions and is worried about the next steps. She knows the gift she was given and what was asked of her. She did it to the best of her ability. She did it with excitement and joy, but also with fear and worry that she wouldn't get it right, it wouldn't be enough, and she would ruin it with her imperfections and humanity. She tried to be a good steward. Was it enough?

"Please, she whispers, I need to hear from You."

As the words leave her lips hope and peace settle over her like a light brush of wings —a gentle blanket of fragrance that permeates and soothes. Familiar goosebumps prick along the nape of her neck and arms. The supernatural is here, a divine encounter. Be still…be still…

Resting in His peace she breathes in the hope of Him. Bree envisions herself lifting up this gift and placing it back into strong, capable, divine hands that know exactly what needs to be done and how He will do it. She remembers the verse in Isaiah 55:11 (NIV) that He showed her when He first gave her this gift: "so is my word that goes out from my mouth: it will not return to me empty, but will accomplish what I desire and achieve the purpose for which I sent it."

His hands receive her gift and the cacophony of voices clamoring for attention, giving advice and opinions are silent now. His will prevails and His voice drowns out all else. This. This is what she's been seeking. Peace that doesn't make sense but still is…this knowing and discernment that speaks to what is and is to come. She needed to remember all the ways He's spoken to her. She needed to be reminded that she is capable of hearing, discerning, and resting in that knowing. Assurance.

Spirit and soul refreshed by her divine appointment in the forest, Bree stays a bit longer, soaking in the healing balm of nature. Her heart feels hopeful. Courage infuses her spirit. She is confident she can discern the next step and the right time to take it. She rests in that hope and wisdom. She will be still and listen to His promises whispered in the wind and dancing through the treetops.

Maple Leaf's Journey

THE AUTUMN WIND breezes through the park singing and snickering as it tosses and turns upon itself. So fickle and capricious! It's going to be a blustery day. The Maple Leaf waits in anticipation as the merry wind threads through her tree branches, dashing her to and fro. Lovely chaos.

All summer she's watched from her shaded bower as blankets were spread under her tree and picnickers relaxed and napped in the warm afternoons. In the early mornings, squirrels and a variety of birds hopped and scurried through her tree branches, busy with their task of finding breakfast.

The Maple Leaf has looked forward to the coming autumn with such excitement! As she grew and filled out in the early spring, she listened to tales from the park trees of the wild adventures that await her once the cooling winds of autumn arrive.

She knows the Creator has a plan for her journey on the autumn wind. She hears Him pass by in the cool evenings, His breath in the flowers, His laughter dancing with the spritely breeze ever with Him. His presence creates ripples of joy and love that He sends forth to do His bidding. Tonight, the Maple Leaf watches Him in fascination as He stops and speaks in heavenly languages over a weathered picnic table under the old pine at the edge of the park. She often sees lone walkers stop and sit at this shaded table—sometimes serene and relaxed, other times crying out pain and worry with or without words. Miracles happen here… Holy ground in a city park.

The day of her long-anticipated journey arrives with full force! As the wild autumn wind blows and gusts through the tree branches, the Maple Leaf feels her hold on the tree loosen and release her. She's off!

The whims of the wind, precisely orchestrated by the Creator, toss and carry her up and down all around the park. Exhilarating! She soars higher and higher, swirling with other leaves caught up in the gusts, then plunges down to brush over benches and playground equipment where she lands near the swings. Busy children run and shriek with joy as they climb, slide, and soar on the swings. Their laughter is full of carefree happiness and boundless energy. Their smiling caregivers enjoy a warm spot in the sun as they sip their coffee, chat, and monitor the goings-on.

Suddenly, in a burst of wind, she is thrown up and away on another gust twirling over the park, swooping and soaring, joining some spent flower blossoms on a ride of their own.

From her vantage point, the Maple Leaf notices a middle-aged woman walking slowly, but with purpose along the gravel path surrounding the park. The woman is making her way to the picnic table under the old pine, the very table the Creator spoke over last night. The Maple Leaf senses the wind slowing and gentling as she descends down, down, floating toward the picnic table alighting on the edge. There is a snap and vibrancy to the air around this table. The supernatural is afoot and it's palpable. The woman sits and sighs deeply. Her eyes are weary. Her trembling shoulders look as if they are carrying a burden that is too heavy to bear. Tears slip down her cheeks as she pours out her sadness, and the deep fear that needles and pricks at her constantly.

She is so tired—tired of carrying a burden that was never hers to carry, tired of expending energy on someone who wounds her heart again and again. She's tired and afraid of the future. The Maple Leaf listens to her heart-cry. The Creator knew the woman would find rest here when He spoke healing, love, and release over it, speaking and prophesying in the language of heaven exactly what her spirit needed. This divine exchange between the hurt and the Healer is the most beautiful, sacred thing the Maple Leaf has ever witnessed. A life healed and restored here under the old pine as His whispers floated on the autumn breeze, His love surrounded her, and the Divine mystery of Him healed her aching heart.

Rising from the picnic table with renewed hope, a gentle smile, and His peace on her shoulders, the beloved woman finishes her walk in the park with a lighter step. The Maple Leaf is full of awe and wonder at all she witnessed. Beautiful. Intentional. Holy Ground.

Understanding that her adventure on the blustery autumn wind is coming to an end, the Maple Leaf senses Him calling and singing to her, as He buoys her up, higher and higher into His glorious presence where angels and heavenly beings dwell.

Raw

THE MORNING VIEW from my kitchen window is filled with shafts of pink and pale orange that stripe the sunrise sky and mix with the slate grey of the cloud cover. It's so quiet and still. The neighbor's fig and plum trees have lost all their leaves. The branches look stark and exposed, stripped of their leaf cover. Raw...

I'm the first one up except for the dog and cats. The house is chilly as the heater begins its task of warming things up. I love the feeling of my warm coffee mug bringing life to my chilled hands. It's comforting. It's soothing. It's routine. I look forward to it every day.

Standing at my kitchen window, watching the Creator paint the sky with even brighter hues and bursts of brilliance, that word raw simmers in my brain. I feel raw this morning. It can be defined as: in its natural state; not yet processed or purified; not analyzed, evaluated, or processed for use.

The Christmas season is over and the new year looms ahead. I always feel off-kilter and unsettled this time of year. The buildup and anticipation, the bright glitter and shine, special food, and the hope of seeing loved ones have worn off and dulled. Putting it all away for next year, the clearing up and cleaning out, the goodbyes and see ya laters await, and it's raw and painful. So much can happen in a year, a month, a minute, and I am not a fan of uncertainty. I try to live in the moment, let go of worry and lean into the blessings and adventures that will come. But it's hard. My emotions are raw and chaotic. They need a resting place. Help, Jesus...

As I watch the morning unfold and attempt to sort my thoughts, a feeling of safety and tucking-in surrounds me. It's beautiful and startling. I know it's You. The comforting words of Psalm 139: 1-2 (NIV) come to my mind: "You have searched me, Lord and you know me. You know when I sit and when I rise; you perceive my thoughts from afar." As Your words soak in, the pent-up emotions and chaos tumble forth. You understand the raw, the chaos, and the frantic, unsettled feelings that don't have a place to land. You are the landing place—the wide-open hands. You are Alpha and Omega, the One who can sort, sift, and make sense of my jumbled thoughts and rawness. You calm and smooth out the unanalyzed, not yet processed natural state of the human heart, and You purify it. It is freeing and cleansing, giving it to You in its raw and mixed-up state.

I don't have to tone it down, gauge the emotional capacity of the one I'm sharing with, diminish myself to protect someone else or use copious amounts of humor to tame it and make it palatable to another. With You, I am just me—the unprocessed feelings, laughter and tears, the nonsense, hope, and fluttering anticipation that watches and waits to see what blessings You will pour out this year.

We need a safe place to just be with Someone who knows every thought, emotion, and the reasons behind each one. It is a beautiful, holy, and sacred thing to be raw. No holding back—no explanations and justifications. The whole of our humanity is in the presence of the One who created every nuance. I never realized how freeing and breathtakingly intimate it is to be raw in the presence of God. It is holy. It is sacred ground.

A High Rock

WRAPPED in her crimson scarf, with her dark green beanie and brown combat boots, Jasmine makes her way to the dirt road winding past her home. Tendrils of black hair wisp and flutter around her cheeks and forehead as she walks.

The air is bracing and chilly, but the hot coffee with cream warms her hands through the lidded thermos.

The crunch of her boots is such a satisfying sound. It's purposeful with meaning and direction. The rhythmic sound is comforting and familiar.

This year has been one of many changes—some welcome and some not, some expected and some blindsiding. Having no control over her life or that of her loved ones is a heavy weight on her raw and tender heart. There is no balance to any of it and she cannot fix or smooth it over. The helplessness piles up leaving her overwhelmed and tired. With every step she visualizes pounding the troubles deep into the dusty country road. She imagines the puffs of dirt and tiny pebbles in her wake floating away on the breeze, but they don't. The troubles just settle into a different spot in her journey.

Making her way along the road Jasmine feels the peace and tranquility of the countryside work its magic. Her tight shoulders and neck release just a bit, her mind focusing on what's around her. Birds chatter in the copse of trees up ahead around the slight bend in the road. There is some marshy land to the right filled with tiny bugs and tasty treats for the morning hunters. It's a happy noise these birds and creatures make as they faithfully trust their Creator to provide. All they need to do is watch, listen, and seek out what He gives.

Passing under the branches of the gnarled oaks, Jasmine notices a change in temperature. The morning sun is temporarily blocked, and the chill air brushes her exposed neck and face. This is how her heart feels—like a shadow has fallen over her spirit, drowning out the light and warmth. It leaves her chilled and exposed. In this shadowy place, she's lost her perspective. Everything seems obscure and vague with too many unknowns.

On the other side of the oak trees a small trail branches off to the right. In the swaying grasses she hears a faint sigh beckoning her to veer off and take the path. "Why not?" she whispers. She's up for adventure.

She has hiked this country lane many times and doesn't remember this particular path. Up ahead it curves to the left around a cluster of small trees. Past the trees, the path drops down, snaking off through the countryside. As the path begins its descent, clusters of large rocks jut out like a shelf with flowering bushes surrounding it. It feels safe and protected. Sheltered.

Fascinated, Jasmine climbs up and sits on the rock shelf. She lets herself breathe in the cool air and feels the warmth of the late autumn sun penetrate her exposed skin. Warmth and protection begin working their way into that shadowy, frozen place in her heart. It's such a cozy feeling of safety.

Looking around, she notices bits of dried leaves and finished flower petals from the nearby bushes strewn about the rock. They spin and shimmy along like random spinners until they float off the rocky edge, following the breeze on their journey. The freedom of these floating petals makes her smile. Oh, to feel so light, so free, so joyful…

The wind picks up, dancing and whispering through the wildflowers around her rock. A gentle peace descends on her shoulders and threads through her hair. The tears she has so fiercely guarded and held at bay fall and flow down her face, splashing the rock like drops from her heart. Each tear holds the name of one she holds dear, of one she loves and desperately wants to protect, wrap up tight, and keep from all harm and violence. But she's tired. Her heart can't contain all the striving, soldiering on, and fixing…it's beyond what she can do. It rips and pulls at her spirit.

As the cleansing flood of tears subsides, Jasmine discovers that in the warm, life-giving sunlight, her tears soak up and evaporate. As a hush falls over the rock a Voice she knows well speaks to her soul. "Let them go, beloved. They are safe. Their names are engraved on the palms of My hands. I have placed you upon a high rock, and you will find rest. I am a shield about you; you are never alone."

Her parched spirit soaks up these whispered words and softens. Her troubled, frantic thoughts slow and dissolve, blown away by the flighty breeze tousling her hair. Sitting on this high rock, safe and tucked away, her heart and soul are open. She has room to breathe. In the place where fear and anxiety dwelled, courage and bravery bloom and flourish. Her captured tears become fragrant, life-giving water cleansing and renewing all that was lost and broken. She will find beauty again. She is confident of this.

As the autumn sun makes its lazy descent, Jasmine heads home. Her feet feel light and confident as she follows the path to the main road. The warmth of the setting sun on her back feels comforting and safe. The protective hand of a Father who is ever vigilant and watchful, who has all things under His control. She can rest now. "…My presence will go with you, and I will give you rest." Exodus 33:14-16 (NIV)

Winter Morning

THE SUN hasn't risen over the foothills yet. My bedroom is still dark. In the piles of blankets on my bed I feel cocooned, warm, and cozy. There is a cat, possibly two, curled and softly purring at the foot of the bed, nestled down and warm. I gingerly wiggle and stretch my feet; either cat could wake and attack my moving foot at any time.

Time to get up—there's hot coffee to make and sip in the quiet, peaceful morning of a silent house. Calm. Soothing.

Coffee in hand, the heat from the mug soaks into my chilly fingers. It feels homey, nostalgic, and something else... Anticipation? Expectation?

The lights from the Christmas tree and mantle glow softly and cheerfully in the still-dark living room. The rustic, wooden nativity scene is backlit with a sweet, warm glow from the tiny lights strung along the small side table where it resides. My mind wanders and contemplates all that this sweet and simple scene portrays. A Savior born, a young mother's joy and fear, shepherds' awe, and angel voices. Miracles. Redemption. Love.

A deep fog descended in the early hours of the morning. All is shrouded, misty, and ethereal. Sounds are muffled and muted. I still my breathing for a moment trying to hear the morning bird song, the gentle lowing of cows in the open space, and squirrels rustling through the damp air. All is silent. It's beautiful, disconcerting, and mysterious. I feel all of that in my chest, my mind, and my spirit.

Sipping the warm coffee, my thoughts wander. So many memories fill my mind around the holidays. Ones that are tucked up out of sight for most of the year but are resurrected and return unbidden as Fall approaches and blends into the frenetic pace and high expectations of the Winter holidays. As much as I long for nostalgia, beauty, and excitement, there are lingering and flitting feelings along the periphery that aren't so merry and bright. Ones that call to mind Dr offices, hospitals, devastating news, and dashed expectations. There are, of course, the happy, joyful memories that bubble to the surface, bringing smiles, laughter, and warm nostalgic feelings, but they are not alone, and the memories vie for prominence in my mind.

Looking out my back window at the swirling, wispy fog it feels disorienting and beautiful all at once, in the covering quietness. Stepping outside, the brisk chill of the damp air is startling. Breathing deeply, the cold air zings and stings my lungs. Invigorating.

Through the mist I see light seeping through as the sun makes its ascent and the rays forge a path in the gloom. It's calming.

It brings a sense of order and relief that not all is murky and diminished; that night and darkness will not last forever—the Light is on its way.

The Light pierces through the veils of murky shadows, bringing hope, joy, and comfort. I imagine the awe, fear, and great hope that the first Light brought to the hills of a sleepy little village so many, many years ago. A Light full of joyful celebration, promises, hope, and protection. That Light is still here. It shines, pierces, and breaks through fog, darkness, and the high, often unattainable expectations we crave during the holiday season.

The Light reminds us that hard, sad, and lonely memories can co-exist with joy, peace, living in the moment, and merriment. The Light calms the swirling expectations with a peace that passes all understanding. Dark crevices of memory are illuminated with healing and comfort when we give the Light permission to enter into it with us. It becomes holy ground. He was there when the hurt happened. He has never left. He understands where the deep need and high expectations come from. He delights with us in the silly, happy times that bring joy and a smile to our faces. And He brings hope, so much hope that says we are not alone and all will be well. Emmanuel, God is with us. The Light in the Darkness, Prince of Peace, Mighty Counselor. Always, everywhere, and in every season.

Shafts of Light

THE GIFTS wait with anticipation in the incense-filled room. The voices of the beloved rise and fall in a constant blend of timbres and tones, each voice precious, seen, and so very loved. The Gifts love to watch the Creator as He gently lifts and listens to each request, praise, and cry for help. Sometimes there are no human words, but utterances of the Spirit as deep calls out to deep. These are the voices of His precious ones. Each one cherished. As He lifts each voice and holds it carefully in His hands, He sings and prophesies over it. The Gifts thrum with excitement as they await His command.

With a nod of His head, Peace is sent forth. Descending from the heavenlies, Peace makes a way through the swirling turbulence of humanity to the dear one asking her Father to please blanket her in His peace. Fear and panic threaten and snicker in the shadows of her mind. Gently surrounding, above and below, Peace wraps up the precious one and whispers the words to her spirit that it was sent forth to proclaim. She feels the soft warmth begin to soothe and soften her fearful heart. Panic recedes and fear bows. It is supernatural, this sending forth as Peace simultaneously, yet personally, ministers to thousands of souls at once—the Father's voice and love flowing down and through and within each of His children. Mystery.

Next to descend on a golden shaft of light is Joy. With excitement, Joy finds the man calling out for relief. He is stuck in the never-ending spiral of his daily grind. He is tired and overwhelmed. He wants to feel alive and energized. He needs to know that life hasn't passed him by, so Joy dashes in with bursts of playfulness, humor, and the beauty of hidden blessings revealed. With the return of his joy, he smiles again and opens his heart to all that life has to offer him.

The sound of the rising voices makes the Father smile. The Gifts are transfixed at how attentive He is to each soul. No one goes unnoticed. No one is lost in the crowd of billions. Every voice is completely unique, designed with forethought and purpose; none better than the other, all equal and perfectly loved. There are times that He weeps with those who mourn. The tears that His beloved cry are never wasted, not one single teardrop. He knows the origin and reason for each one. He meticulously collects and places them in lovely crystal jars that have an eternal purpose and plan. He speaks over them in heavenly utterances. Tears will not be wasted.

The next Gifts sent forth are Protection and Healing. These two often travel together. They descend on a powerful beam of light piercing evil and darkness. These Gifts find the ones ensnared and tangled in chains, fear, and illness. The Father infuses these Gifts with His authority, power, and love. Chains break, strongholds crumble, illnesses flee, and darkness bows. Gentleness and Mercy follow Protection and Healing as hearts, souls, and bodies are healed, restored, and led into His Light.

Discernment and Wisdom respond to His command and travel on gentle shafts of light seeking those who are lost, alone, overwhelmed by choices, and clamoring world-voices. These Gifts infuse the overwhelmed soul with calm, direction, and clarity straight from the Father's heart. The webs and twisty-looking paths that shroud the way forward are made clear as the debris and obstacles of self-reliance are rolled away. Trust accompanies Discernment and Wisdom, as those coming out of the shadows need Trust to clearly hear and follow His voice.

Patiently waiting, Rest is summoned and joyfully descends in light infused with lovely colors. It flows like a sparkling creek carefully washing away the busyness and exhaustion that covers so many of the beloved. The weariness of fixing, controlling, worrying, and rehearsing piles up and sticks like a balm of good works gone rancid. In the beginning, the balm feels soothing and necessary, but as peace and joy are sacrificed by the doing and the helping, it becomes suffocating and immobilizing. How beautiful it is to see the caked-on debris slough off in the stream of living water that beckons the weary one to rest in green pastures. Victory.

From His omnipresent vantage point, the Creator watches and is pleased as His love-gifts, in radiant light, descend continuously and purposefully to His beloved. He intimately knows where every shaft of light is going and declares that these Gifts will not return to Him void but will accomplish all that He desires and declares.

The Country Chapel

THE WEATHERED WHITE WOOD of the simple spire comes into view as I crest the gentle hill.

The narrow dirt road leading to the country chapel is overgrown with tufts of sturdy grasses and haphazard rocks. It's rutted and a bit uneven from years of weather, shoes, and tires making their way to church.

The land around the chapel is wild and untamed. Nature has reclaimed this place and surrounded it with beauty, as if cradling the abandoned chapel in lovely colors and peace, so much peace. It feels protected and safe. The Lord is here.

Tall, wispy flowers and assorted meadow grasses bend and sway as a light breeze darts through, bringing movement and faint whisperings of years gone by.

An old pine tree rises up just behind and to the right of the old chapel. The branches are thick and heavy, with a few quirky curves to its old trunk. The old tree has seen and heard so much life, death, joy, and sorrow. The tattered remnants of a rope swing sway and shift with the breeze. Visions of ponytails flying behind the swinger with shrieks of joy as the swing sails higher and higher! Freedom!

Looking up, I see leaves, sticks, and a piece of bright red yarn entwined and fashioned into a sturdy nest settled into the crook of a branch. Humanity may have abandoned this country chapel, but nature still finds shelter and a home here.

Taking a seat on a weathered stone bench under the tree, I imagine these pine branches shading long tables of cold, home-made lemonade, tasty potluck dishes, and desserts on a warm Sunday afternoon as congregants share a meal and life together. If I listen closely, I hear muted laughter, the sharing of gossip, and recipes passed down through the years. Those family recipes will make an appearance at every potluck gathering. Belonging.

Becoming more accustomed to the sounds of silence, I hear bird song and buzzing bugs along with the creak and groan of the old pine settling and shifting with old age. A fluffy, grey squirrel spies on me as it chatters and flicks its tail. One could sit here all day letting the imagination and nostalgia go where they will…

I make my way to the offset wooden steps of the chapel that shift under my feet. The wooden door's paint is peeling, and the bottom has been gnawed and scratched by a creature seeking shelter.

Inside the chapel the hush and silence are palpable. High windows are covered in dust and streaks, with a few broken and missing panes. The light streaming in is lovely and warm—like an invitation to come and rest.

There are ten rows of off-kilter pews on each side of the chapel with a few missing or cracked in places. A tattered red-leather hymnal lies on the edge of one. Some of the pages have been nibbled off and perhaps taken as bedding for a small creature that found safety here.

Moving between the rows, I notice one pew with initials carved into the wood: *KC was here*. Another has a stick horse and flowers etched into it. *Lorraine loves James* is written in orange pen on the back of another pew with some little hearts surrounding the words. Life was lived here.

The altar is simple and pure on its raised-up flooring. It appears to be handmade and sturdy. It's beautiful. Echoes of sermons, wedding vows, and funeral memorials whisper and float on the still, dust-moted air. The chapel may be abandoned but it's holy and alive with memories.

I sit for a bit in the front pew allowing the peace, mystery, and silence of this old chapel to speak and heal. It does. The supernatural is all around. It can be felt in the slight shiver that pricks the back of the neck and dances along the spine. There is no room for fear here; it's lovely, divine, and healing. Beautiful.

The light shifts as the day moves along. I head to the side door leading out to the left. It's loose on rusty hinges and makes a squeaking noise as I push it open and go out.

A lopsided picnic bench sits in the shade of an old, gnarled cherry tree. The legs are hidden by the meadow grasses—the keepers of this place. Resting in the shade, I take in the weathered boards, streaked windows, and lonely cross that sits atop the small spire of this country chapel. I'm struck with the thought that the Father met with His beloved within those walls. He healed, loved, and wept with them. He rejoiced, danced, and comforted them. The sacred holiness of it still permeates and flits within these abandoned walls. But we mustn't try to contain Him inside physical walls, exclusivity, strict rules, or joyless routine. No! He is found under the gnarled old tree where someone sat pouring out their deepest heart wounds and pain. He heard every word, healed, and exchanged the pain for joy and peace. He did this as birds sang, wildflowers soothed, and the breeze took the prayers and cries, tossing them up into His ever-open hands to receive, heal, and restore. He isn't tame, safe, or containable. His love is fierce, wild, joy-filled, and all-consuming. He can be found within the walls of a sweet country chapel, but just as often I find Him in the wild places with dancing wildflowers, leafy trees, creatures, and breathtaking beauty.

My time here is complete. So many lessons learned from the old and abandoned. This country chapel with its divine murmurs and lonely beauty spoke volumes to me as I sat in the memories, nostalgia, and quiet. This old chapel and the nature that cradles and shelters it healed, comforted, and spoke to my soul in ways a spoken word never could. Divine whispers float and swirl all around us—may we have the ears to hear it and hearts to discern it.

Storms

LOOKING OUT my front windows to the north I see a storm brewing. Clouds in various shapes and sizes in varying degrees of grey, black, and white are simmering and building. They appear motionless, but they're not. The wind chimes on the patio are strumming and singing, growing more insistent as the wind announces the approaching storm. Rain and wind are coming. Will there be thunder and lightning? I notice the absence of bird song and chatter. The bare-bones apple tree branches are filled with little birds watching and waiting. Nature knows...

When the weather forecasters display their satellite-generated models of atmospheric pressure, wind, moisture, and all the variables that make up a storm, it can bring a sense of security in knowing what's coming, and how to plan and predict. Sometimes these predictions are spot on and other times not.

Watching for this storm to make its entrance reminds me of life. There are times when all the little hairs on the back of the neck and arms stand on end and our discernment and awareness are heightened. We feel a storm approaching. We are alert and aware of every changing nuance in our atmosphere. We watch body language and hear what is and isn't said. We are hyper-aware that something is wrong as we observe our surroundings. The unsettled feeling of knowing something is coming but not knowing how to prepare stirs up feelings of fear and urgency into a thick brew of panicked helplessness.

Other times, due to circumstances, conversations, or a diagnosis received, we know what is coming and try to predict, sometimes with accuracy and sometimes not, what the outcome will be. Having that knowledge brewing in our thoughts can be exhausting as we rehearse and attempt to control what's coming. But we really can't, can we?

Our limited humanity is frightening and fragile. We desperately want to control and carefully order our lives. We want peace and happiness and attempt to forge for ourselves a chaos-free zone that protects us and shuts out all things harmful and terrible. We might succeed for a bit in keeping at bay all that howls and thrashes outside, but there are cracks—flaws in our construction and the storm knows the way inside. Sometimes it patiently waits, prodding and poking the infrastructure, testing, and observing where the design flaws are hiding. Little by little it oozes in causing small bits of erosion and damage that we don't notice immediately until chunks of our carefully constructed barriers begin crumbling and falling away.

Other times it strikes so violently and fast that our safe bubble pops with terrifying suddenness, and we are left in a ruin of rubble and disaster with no idea how to rebuild. Blindsided.

Amid all this ruin is Hope. Jesus.

He's the Master Designer. He is the Light that breaks through all darkness and commands it to flee. He's done it before, is doing it, and will do it again. Why He permits the storms and darkness to enter our bubbles, I don't know. I have cried, raged, and demanded answers for the bubble-breaking storms I have endured. I do know that He wants to take the hurt, rage, and heartbreak from us. He is the only one who can take the wounded devastation and rebuild those ruins into something breathtaking and beautiful. It becomes sacred ground. It is Holy. What He rebuilds is strong, graceful, thankful, and full of hope. He positions us to be light to another who finds themselves in the midst of a storm. He takes ashes and gives beauty. He takes mourning and gives joy. He takes heaviness and despair and replaces it all with a spirit of praise and peace, as is said in Isaiah 61:3 (TLB): "To all who mourn in Israel he will give: beauty for ashes; joy instead of mourning; praise instead of heaviness. For God has planted them like strong and graceful oaks for his own glory."

Sometimes the strongholds we've built must be torn down for us to experience all that is waiting for us on the other side of the storm. Way maker, miracle worker, promise keeper, light in the darkness. That is Jesus and He is our hope—our true anchor in the storm.

The Invitation

STEAM from her Paris Blend tea dances in the breeze, floating in through the open patio door. It is a pretty morning. The air has that perfect blend of crisp coolness with an undercurrent of warmth. It's going to be another lovely fall day.

The Japanese Maple in the backyard is just beginning to turn. Crystal's hard work re-doing the garden is paying off with bright bursts of oranges, yellows, and reds as the Mums proudly display their colors.

Stepping outside to fill the bird feeders, she whistles and calls to the doves, crows, finches, and sparrows that grace her yard. Crystal loves that they wait for her every morning. They trust her and count on her. Sometimes she feels like the birds, squirrels, and neighborhood cats are her only friends, the only ones looking forward to seeing her. They notice if she's off schedule or away from the house. These critters don't care whether her hair is wild and untamable, or if her sweats have a hole or two. That longing in her heart for someone to accept her and be excited to see her with her quirks, flaws, and humor pops up again. Is there anyone out there who will enjoy her company without pretense, expectations, and judgment? She wants to belong.

Finishing her egg white omelet and toast, Crystal hears rustling at her front door. She wonders what her cats, Dixie and Dude, have gotten into this time. Dixie lounges on the back of the recliner while Dude investigates a cream-colored envelope that's been pushed under her front door. Lifting it up, there is nothing telling on this envelope except for her name, Crystal, in a script that seems familiar but that she can't quite place. It is heavy, good-quality paper. Hmmm... Holding the envelope, a gentle feeling of peace settles over her shoulders and a lovely warmth spreads through her hands, arms, and chest and hovers there, right over her heart. It brings tears to her eyes though she isn't sure why. Anticipation rises over what this simple envelope holds as she carefully lifts the flap. Crystal slides a crisp, iridescent card out of the envelope and sees that it's a hand-written invitation in that same beautiful script.

"Your presence is requested at my family banquet. Come as you are, Crystal. You are enough. Follow the Light, you will know where to go."

An invitation to a family banquet? She's never been invited to anything like this before. She's uncertain what to think and do. What will she wear? It said, "Come as you are..." There isn't a return address or a location listed. How will she know what the Light looks like or where to find it? The anxiety trying to push in and distract her slowly ebbs and fades as she gazes at the envelope. There is something about the handwriting that soothes her mind and spirit. That warm feeling of safety and peace is still there, enfolding her heart, reminding her that she knows the way. Whispers…

In faded jeans and her favorite green shirt, Crystal takes a final look in the mirror. Her long auburn hair caught up in a sleek bun looks neat and tidy. Will she fit in? The invitation says she is enough…

She feels an interesting pull toward the lake in her neighborhood. As she walks, random words to a song she sang in a church long ago flit through her mind… *All who are thirsty…*

Approaching the lake, she sees the warm autumn sunlight filtering and shimmering through the branches of the willow tree. It's breathtaking. "Follow the Light…" the invitation said.

Reaching the tree, she sits on the familiar bench; the warmth of the afternoon and the peaceful shushing of the lake lull and quiet her mind. This is her favorite spot. It is tucked in and private. Her secret place. The breeze moving through the willow branches sounds like a soft whisper…

Her breathing slows…

A slight murmuring and rustling sound to her left catches her attention. Looking around, she notices a rustic wooden table. Its simplicity is beautiful. The rough-hewn wood appears to be hand-crafted by a Master carpenter. It's stunning as it glows and beckons to her to come closer. Drawing near, Crystal sees that the chairs around this table have velvety cushions of bright purple with gold thread woven throughout.

Taking a closer look at the table, she sees her name, Crystal, on a lovely blue place card. Her name is hand-written in the same script as the invitation. This is her place, and she sits down. The softness of the bright purple cushion envelopes her in such comfort. The faint scent of honey and something wild and fresh waft around the table and chairs.

There are other place cards around the table in a rainbow of vivid colors. Each one has a name and a unique script. The space to her left is reserved for Jazz and the one to her right is for Juan Carlos. Interestingly enough the table appears small, but it isn't. There are so many seats and so many names. Family.

The other invitees begin to arrive with the same look on their faces that Crystal imagines is on her own. Awe, uncertainty, and hesitation, yet a longing for community and joy mixed into one. Josh sits down across from her, joined by Emma, Miriam, Yosef, Carmen, Wren, and Braden. A bit further down Damien, Paul, Grace, and Vincent find their places. She looks in fascination at each person. The mix of humanity at this table is beautiful. Everyone is so unique and different—life experiences that are intentional and diverse yet connected in a deep and perfect way. Belonging.

Bringing her focus back to the table, Crystal sees the delicacies arranged in front of them. It appears random at first glance, yet there is perfect order here. Dishes overflowing with fruit, earthen-ware jars filled to the top with honey, and baskets of fragrant, warm bread are interspersed along the table. At each place is a tall, thin glass with mysterious etchings and symbols carved into them. These glasses are filled with clear water that sparkles, shimmers, and dances in the Light that filters through the willow branches. This water captivates her with its absolute clarity and unique fragrance that flows, caresses, and feels like love. Each guest lifts their glass in unity and drinks deeply; it feels like healing. "All who are thirsty…"

The Host of this extraordinarily beautiful banquet is here. This is Holy ground, and He sits among His guests. Supernaturally, each one of them holds His undivided attention. He speaks, heals, reveals, and lavishes joy, peace, and belonging to all who are at His banquet. They are all enough. There is no one at the head and no one at the foot. Every place is equal, chosen, and important. In His mystery and wisdom, He is everywhere at once ministering exactly what is needed. No one is taking over, minimizing, drowning out, or elevated over another. They all belong because they are all His. Agendas, politics, and man-made idols are not found here. They are not welcome and have been denied access to this family banquet. Ahhh…the peace, beauty, and tranquility of a table set for everyone. A taste of heaven…

As His gaze penetrates her soul, the pain and despair of feeling like an outsider and the trauma of rejection and loneliness flow out of her heart into His hands. As He speaks and sings over these things in an ancient language of Love, Crystal's heart is cleansed. It feels new, tender, and ready to receive Him. He is enough. Her lungs fill with His breath. Her blood flows with His healing. She is ok. She is safe. She belongs to Him. She belongs to this wildly diverse family seated around His banquet table. There is a place for her.

The whisper of faint singing rouses her from sleep. How long has she been here? She doesn't remember falling asleep. This is the place where she comes to talk to Him. A playful breeze tickles her neck and fluffs her hair. As she wakes and stretches, Crystal notices something sparkling in the reeds along the water's edge. Curious, she moves in for a closer look. It's a piece of gold thread. Smiling, she picks it up and holds it in her hands. Memories fill her mind and hide themselves in her heart—a blessing-laden table, acceptance, and her name written on a place card at His banquet table.

Always

"AND SURELY I AM with you always, to the very end of the age."
Matthew 28:20 (NIV)

Always. Without fail. For eternity. For keeps.

Enjoying my morning coffee as I watch the garden waking
up, Jesus is here. He's here as I listen to the bird-chatter and the
soft breeze tinkling my wind chimes. The melody is gentle and
peaceful. The birds and squirrels go about their tasks filled with
trust, instinctively knowing their Father will provide for them.
I'm not alone, even in the simple, ordinary routine of morning
coffee and birdsong. Comforting. Always.

Walking in my neighborhood or around the duck pond, He's
here with me watching the seasons change, delighting in my awe
over the gorgeous colors His creation displays. Beauty. Forever.

Going about my day filled with errands, appointments,
puttering, and gardening, He's here giving encouragement and
energy to finish all that goes into taking care of those things and
people He has entrusted me with. Presence. For keeps.

When fear raises its ugly head, making an appearance in circumstances involving loved ones that I cannot control or predict, Jesus is here. He understands the fear and uncertainty simmering in my heart. He sees the worst-case scenarios I conjure up that give place to overthinking and worry. He speaks soothing peace and divine protection over all of it. He is aware of every nuance of human emotion and the messy chaos that comes from living on this planet. Yet He never leaves me alone. Safety. For eternity.

In the lonely and hidden places of my soul and yours, where bleeding wounds and feeble attempts at self-healing live, we find Jesus fully present. He isn't looking away in embarrassment. He isn't disgusted or done with us. He is fully invested, present, and active. The compassion and mercy flowing from Him into these wounded places, if we'll let Him in, is sacred. It is holy ground. Miracles happen here. Strongholds are demolished, captives are set free, and new life begins. Heavenly battles are waged over us, and He wins. He always wins. Our pain is never too much or minimized and glossed over with rote Christan-ese and trite, shallow words. He speaks renewal, healing, and blessings over these deep places and shouts victory over what He heals. The songs He sings into our hearts soften the hard places as His blood and provision course through us. He is with us always, for eternity, for keeps, without fail to the very end of the age.

Peace

The Creek in the Hollow

THERE IS a little tucked-away hollow with a bubbly creek running through it. You can find it if you listen.

A lively jaunt through some meadow grass will get you there.

Gentle willow trees sway and beckon, "Come, and sit a while."

The only sounds are nature's chatter and the swish of grasses and wildflower stems as they rustle against booted feet, making their way to the water.

A slight dip in the path and you are there.

The gurgling creek splashes happily over some stones and fallen, decaying branches. The rivulets and tiny waterfalls rush and dash through the haphazard obstacle course.

On the opposite side of the creek, the paws of the early risers have left their unique imprints. Breakfast starts early in the hollow.

The bank of the creek is dotted with a variety of wildflowers, all adding their color and charm to the hollow. Small yellow flowers on their tall, leggy stems love the chaos of the breeze that randomly tosses them about. The purple-blue flowers growing close to the ground create a happy, fragrant carpet with soft leaves that soothe tired feet. Bold white flowers lift their faces upward to the patches of sun filtering through the drooping willow branches.

Downstream the water slows and takes on a lazy pace. Widening into a small pool gently flowing around the roots of an old tree, one imagines what creek dwellers make this restful pool their home. The water may appear calm, but life is busy and active underneath the slow ripples.

At the edge, tiny fish dart in and out of watery shadows, and the quick boatman skips over the quiet water. The grumpy, orange crawdad silently waits under a ledge of roots, motionless and spying. Nothing gets past this watchman of the creek.

Little plip-plop sounds come from the far edge of the pool—small frogs, perhaps? The tiny gnats and other flyers that flit and hover over the water make a tasty meal for hungry frogs and turtles.

The tranquility of nature with its calming rhythms of sound, light, and timeless order, soothes and quiets a restless soul. The pull of it is timeless and constant.

Accepting the willow trees' invitation to sit for a while, the weight of all you have been carrying lifts and floats—up, up to the One who gives rest and peace. He is there in the light that sifts through the branches providing warmth and safety. He is in the cooling breezes that kiss and skim the skin. The Divine whispers and sings all around you as He leads you beside still waters and restores your soul.

Expectations

THE CLAMOR of expectations can be overwhelming. Sometimes they are of my own making, that inner voice telling me what I "should" do and all the ways I am falling short. Then there are the external expectations from family, friends, and groups we belong to telling us we "must" …whatever the current trend. The pressure can feel heavy and unrealistic. Burnout lurks, biding its time, knowing that before long something has to give. Often it is me and you.

Expectation is sly in the way it approaches. It doesn't always barge in wild and obnoxious. Sometimes it creeps in slowly and methodically, as inch by inch, the overwhelm advances. At times it looks flashy and exciting bringing an energy of anticipation, progress, and fitting in. Other times it pops up on the radar as something noble needing attention, something worthwhile and necessary. How well expectation understands the human heart! Getting ahead, working to exhaustion, people-pleasing and relegating ourselves to last on the list, to name a few. Challenging this mindset isn't second nature. It's a process and a change in perspective. There is a delicate balance between success, concern for our fellow humans, and prioritizing self-care with essential seasons of rest and peace.

As expectation slithers in, those things that are important for our health and well-being tend to be downplayed and wither. With energy going to nebulous societal expectations, peace, and contentment often run dry. Things enjoyed and required for recharging the mind, body, and spirit, for simply being happy, become scarce. This is not the heart of the Father. This constant striving and relentless giving invites stress and panic as our thoughts become anxious and dissatisfied. All the working and planning are never enough.

This is where Jesus, the Prince of Peace, whispers to us in the sunrise that greets us as we fix our morning coffee: "Slow down! Savor the warm deliciousness a bit longer." He enchants us with snappy breezes, a lovely fall afternoon, and restful friends. Joy and contentment move to the forefront as the bossy demands of humanity are put in their proper place. Scriptures hidden in the heart surface and speak as we turn toward Him with the reminder to "Cast all your anxiety on Him because He cares for you."[1]

Living our dreams does not require us to lose ourselves in the doing. We were not created to "do" to the point of burnout. Jesus wants us to enjoy sunsets at the beach, good coffee, and time with Him as He speaks what our parched spirits crave. We can rest without guilt seeping in to taint the peace of His presence.

---

1   1 Peter 5:7 (NIV)

"But the fruit of the Spirit is love, joy, peace, forbearance, kindness, goodness, faithfulness, gentleness and self-control. Against such things there is no law."[2]

It is wise to let go of expectations that take away our joy, faith, and trust. Those expectations are not from Him.

"Peace I leave with you; My peace I give you. I do not give to you as the world gives. Do not let your hearts be troubled and do not be afraid."[3]

2   Galatians 5:22-23 (NIV)

3   John 14:27 (NIV)

The Ember

It's ALWAYS BEEN THERE, carefully placed as you were sung into existence in the silence and holiness of the Creator's workplace.

Attention, such detailed, undivided attention, was given to you as all your lovely parts, pieces, and quirks were formed, shaped, and worked into His masterpiece.

Chance and random chaos have no place here.

Cherubim wings flutter and sigh as the ember is plucked from the coals in the Most Holy Place.

Selected with forethought and care, the ember is tucked gently into your soul. His breath fans it into a small but steady flame. Heaven watches as it grows and twists, snugly fitting into the place created for it.

Nothing by accident.

This ember is precious. The Father gently and purposefully tends to it night and day, minute by minute. Divine whispers—deep calls to deep.

A tapestry of life and divine appointments are woven and entwined all around and about you. Their sole purpose is fanning this ember with Holy breath, encounters with angels and fellow humans with beautiful burning embers, not unlike your own.

The ember is designed with a divine connection to the Father, a constant soul-longing for divine encounters, conversations, and simply Him. His presence, His breath, His gaze is always enough and more than enough.

It can dim, this ember of yours, seeming to barely flicker as circumstances and other humans vie for that place in your soul. It can feel lonely and grim.

What fans the ember back into brilliance and strength is time with the Creator, the one whose breath and love prophesied and sang over you and called you from what wasn't into one fashioned in His image.

You can find Him everywhere. He is among the Redwoods as you breathe in the scent of old growth or along the beach as relentless waves take fear and worry away with each ebb and flow of the tide. He is found in the mundane tasks of living, sipping warm coffee, or laughing with a dear friend.

How close He is to you! Listen and you will hear His whispers and songs. Simply seek Him and wait with expectation. The ember constantly searches for that divine connection. It knows where to find Him for a beautiful rekindling of the flame.

Worry Webs

SHAFTS OF MORNING LIGHT shine through the pine branches and cast shifting patterns of shadow and light on Cassidy's bedroom wall. Another day is here. All is quiet in the rambling farmhouse. Her cats, Violet and Panther, raise sleepy heads in response to her feet rustling the quilt they are snuggled on together. In the distance a rooster crows his daily greeting to the rising sun. Predictable.

Leaning against the counter by the sink, Cassidy gazes out the kitchen window at her terraced backyard. The birdbaths are full of clear water and the summer flowers are in full bloom. Fragrant and soothing. The cats know the morning routine well and are waiting for breakfast, their gentle head-butts becoming more insistent. The smell of her morning coffee brewing brings her happiness. The stronger the better!

This is her favorite time of the day. Early morning usually reminds her of new adventures, hidden treasures, and second chances. It's a clean slate to create and color the day with hope and the promises of blessings. But she's struggled this past week to find that joy and see any blessings. The simple things that often bring her pleasure and peace feel just out of reach and elusive.

That first rich, earthy sip of coffee lifts her spirits a bit, but even this tried-and-true morning ritual is falling flat. It's frustrating and disheartening.

Taking her coffee to the backyard she sits in her favorite lounge chair. Her spot is nestled under a Jasmine arbor. The bright white flowers are so tiny and dainty, yet they offer the most beautiful fragrance.

As she stretches out, Cassidy's mind begins to wander and turns toward the unwelcome thoughts and scenarios that seem to be on repeat lately. They are intrusive and bothersome. Sticky…

She worries over the future of her small business, the health of a family member, and an ongoing disagreement with a dear friend that leaves a sad, bitter taste in her mouth. These worries churn in her mind like a chaotic dance with no clear steps. Nothing comes together the way she envisioned, and the way forward is cloudy and obscure. The debris and clutter of overthinking sticks to and tangles up the passion and dreams He breathed into her spirit. The bold, sly voices of Confusion and Panic poke and tease her mind. Soon the sticky webs of worry and unbelief begin to wrap and weave themselves around her heart and mind, pining her in place and preventing her from moving forward. She feels trapped. Tears prick at the back of her eyes before sliding down her cheeks, falling onto her arms.

"Please, Lord, will you help me?"

Cassidy isn't sure how much time has passed when she hears the faint, cheerful sound of her tinkling wind chimes and the busy fussing and clucking of the neighbor's chickens. Peaceful.

The sweet, heady scent of flowers and a deliciously spicy mix of herbs and something heavenly perfumes the air around her lounge chair. As her muscles relax and her busy mind slows, Cassidy feels His presence in the garden and such comforting peace. It blows over and around her as she recalls His gentle whispers of protection, acceptance, and love. She knows His voice. She feels it resonate deep within as He begins His work of clearing out and untangling her from the sticky webs of unbelief and worry. "Help my unbelief," she whispers. "I trust You with me."

There is pain at times in the clearing out, but His compassion flows into the wounds, and the relief she feels is glorious. She wants to live life letting go of all she can't control and enjoy the contentment of living in the moment. She wants a life spent capturing glimmers and glimpses of the divine as He whispers and calls out blessings and hope to surround and enfold her.

She remembers all of the answered prayers and divine encounters—a way was made when she couldn't see one, and blessings appeared where she least expected them. He turned things meant for evil into good and things meant to harm her to bring life. As her mind is released from the frantic worry webs that consumed and wounded her, Cassidy's favorite verse gently settles in her mind - "For I am convinced that neither death nor life, neither angels nor demons, neither the present nor the future, nor any powers, neither height nor depth, nor anything else in all creation, will be able to separate us from the love of God that is in Christ Jesus our Lord."[4]

He is the Divine Artist creating beauty, hope, and promise in her spirit. He nurtures and tends to what He's created with fierce joy, purpose, and a dash of divine mystery.

Hebrews 11:1 (NIV): "Now faith is confidence in what we hope for and assurance about what we do not see."

---

4   Romans 8:38-39 (NIV)

Distractions

HAVE YOU NOTICED that as we move closer to our divine calling unexpected distractions, unresolved issues, and time hogs begin popping up seemingly out of nowhere? Vying for our attention, the distractions attempt to drown out the Whisper that calls us into our passion and purpose. They work hard to entice us away with superficial temptations, rabbit holes of worry, and fear of the unknown. Their voices are seductive and sweet, breathing promises they will not keep.

As we strive after their lies it will never be enough. The burden will overwhelm and constantly occupy our thoughts. The goal of these distractions is to minimize the difference we will make in our spheres of influence. They attempt to derail the divine plans prophesied over us as we were formed in the secret place of heaven. "The thief comes only to steal and kill and destroy; I have come that they may have life, and have it to the full."[5]

5   John 10:10 (NIV)

Breakthroughs and divine exchanges happen when we move toward our higher purpose. Heavenly battles are fought and won as the Father removes situations and people that deter and detract from His plans. He filters them out through the shield of His presence and protection. Busyness, people-pleasing, perfectionism, and self-reliance must bow and retreat at the authority of His voice and the command of His gaze.

Our Father provides carefully thought-out opportunities for us to rest. These times of refreshment allow us to live in a place of joy and fulfillment so His plans for us can breathe, thrive, and take shape. We are infused with confidence and strength to continue our journey as distractions fall by the wayside. May we find that place of rest in His presence, welcome it in, and invite it to stay a while.

Strength

I COLLECT coffee mugs. It makes me happy to open my cupboard, see all the mugs with their various pictures and words, go with my gut feeling, and choose a mug for my morning coffee. Perhaps it's fanciful, but often the mug I choose directly correlates to my mood or what might be going on in life at the moment.

Lately, the ones I've chosen reflect a combination of peace, hope, and strength. This morning, I chose a simple white mug with STRENGTH. on the front of it. Something about the quiet, simple words written in all capital letters with that final period at the end sang out to me. It isn't fancy and eye-catching. It is quiet, firm, fierce, and unwavering—*STRENGTH.*

Strength is defined in so many ways. I find the way this word resonates fascinating, as it makes itself comfortable through a season of sifting and sorting relationships, through the ebb and flow of life, and my relationship with Jesus.

Sometimes we imagine strength as needing heft—to be loud and obvious, and it is, in some ways. Physical strength is something I work at. I want to be strong as I navigate aging by doing the outdoorsy things that I love—hiking, camping, and gardening. Isaiah 46:4 (TLB) is such a kind and safe verse, assuring us that even when our physical strength does wane, we will be safe and secure. "I will be your God through all your lifetime, yes, even when your hair is white with age. I made you and I will care for you. I will carry you along and be your Savior."

I am blessed in this current season of life as a military mom to have found courageous women to connect with and befriend. These women understand how exciting, difficult, pride-filled, and terrifying this season is with unknowns, sudden changes, and times of silence—trusting that "no news is good news" and believing God has our soldiers in His hands. Witnessing the strength these women display gives me hope, strength, and a safe place. I am grateful for them. This strength is silent and often unseen but incredibly powerful. The Master Weaver knew our paths would intersect in this season of our lives. He knew how important and vital these connections and friendships would be and the strength we would glean from each other in this shared experience.

As life seasons come and go I find there is a quiet yet fierce strength in letting go, setting boundaries, and sometimes losing relationships you were sure would last a lifetime. This strength is tough because it is born from pain, loss, and heartache. But, if we rest in the assurance that our Father is weaving something beautiful from the pain and lovely surprises He plants along the way, we see that He is strengthening and preparing us for the next season.

There is another type of strength I've found as my life with Jesus continues to evolve. Acceptance. I embrace that I am unique and so are you. I commune with Him in the specific way He created me. This infuses me with hope, strength, and joy. It will not look the same for you and that's a wonderful thing. I have spent too much time and life draining energy putting myself in a religious box that isn't meant for me, oftentimes feeling a check in my spirit that something is off—that I'm not living and being who God designed me to be. Authentic.

There is strength in accepting and nurturing the way you are created to do life with Jesus. It isn't our strength but His that will flow, renew our hope, and restore our tired and frazzled souls—strengthening us for the path He is waiting to walk with us. I hope we will let go, seek out, and enjoy the journey. I believe we will be surprised and delighted to see the strength we will find in unexpected places. Divine whispers are all around, waiting for us to be strong in the silence and waiting as we discover the beauty and hope in the adventures ahead.

Light

THE FIRST GENTLE RAYS of sunrise bathe the cluster of Redwoods in a pale, quiet glow. The forest air is crisp and clean as it sheds the last vestiges of night.

Nature's early risers watch and wait. They are eager to greet the new day with gossip and chatter. The early light calls them to bring their songs and joy to the new morning. The undergrowth is full of rustles and kicked-about leaves as the hunt for seeds and insects begins.

Shadows and light play off of each other, illuminating swaths of the leafy forest floor as the sun makes its ascent. Sunbeams filtering through the branches catch and backlight tiny dust motes trapped in the air. It feels supernatural how the rays of light are so concentrated, yet gentle, like a divine spotlight that pierces and penetrates, exposing everything to the pure, beautiful light. Each beam highlights and dances over the branches, trunks, and leafy bushes, casting an ethereal, otherworldly glow to the waking forest. One might expect angels to move in this mysterious light. Whispers of the divine abound.

The crooked curve of a branch, the rough edges of tree bark, mossy growth, and choking poison ivy that entwines as it creeps up the trees are laid bare in the light. Everything stands out in stark relief. Even dead, cracked branches that are brittle, hard, and dull are bathed in light, and a kind of loveliness is restored. Beauty is found in unexpected places…

There are no secrets here. Nothing is hidden. The rough, sharp scars, the dead and ugly pieces, and random vines threatening to suffocate the beauty of the trees are naked and exposed in the lovely, glowing light. Holy.

Transformation happens in the Light. All is revealed and can be made whole again. We find beauty in the dead, scarred places when the One who pierces the darkness with His breath, His gaze, and His thoughts turn His eyes to those unlovely parts that we so desperately want to hide. Shame is exposed and covered with grace. Wounds are bound and healed as life and prophesy are breathed over them. He makes beautiful things out of the dark, hidden places. Scars show perseverance and victory, dead places are pruned and healed, curves and bumps become testimony, and strangling vines are exposed and burned away in the Light.

His Light can feel harsh, painful, and exposing. It takes courage to stand in it and let the Light do its healing work. But the end result will reap untold, eternal benefits. Joy will come in the morning, when the Morning Star covers and bathes our raw and vulnerable parts with soft, healing, lovely Light.

Changing Direction

Do you ever experience those days, weeks, or months when specific life circumstances have no solid solutions? Where there appears to be no way over, around or through a particular issue?

Not long ago, I was feeling this acutely with frustration and weariness, settling in for what felt like a long and exhausting ride. I was tired of myself and my thoughts mulling things over in exactly the same way and finding no joy, relief, or solution.

There is a park that I love to walk through, especially in the fall. There is something about the way the light slips and shines through the trees. The colors moving through the leaves paint such a hopeful picture, like something is just around the corner out of sight. Anticipation.

Around and around the park I went, following the same path greeting fellow walkers, joggers, and meander-ers. The joy of dogs chasing balls, sniffing after squirrels, and frisking in the cooling fall air felt so calming and happy. Some of the tension in my soul softened and released. I had room to breathe. I noticed peace and a bit of joy seeping in, crowding out the fret, worry, and control that was trying hard to establish dominance. The autumn sun on my face, the crisp air, and the beauty of the park were working their magic.

I distinctly remember rounding a curve in the path. The shade of a big, old oak tree bathed me in cool, sweet air as I stepped into its shade. As I felt the abrupt change from warmth to the cool refreshment of shade, I felt a Whisper nudge my heart saying, "Change directions." I know this Voice. This Voice has spoken to me, prophesied, and sung over me, healed and restored me so many times, in so many circumstances that to listen to it is second nature.

I stopped and stood in the shade for a few minutes and then I changed direction. "What are you saying to me, God?" I whispered. "I'm watching, I'm listening."

Walking in a different direction along this familiar path, I noticed that things looked different than they did when I was going the other way. I could see the other side of the trees and the way the light looked different peeking through branches that I couldn't see before. I saw a bird's nest and squirrels nibbling at pinecones which had been obscured from view. There was a group of older men sitting in a circle in their weathered lawn chairs with tired dogs lolling and stretching out as they chatted and laughed together. I couldn't see them when I was walking in the other direction because they were hidden from view by a large cluster of trees. Seeing them there enjoying their dogs and long-time friendship made me smile.

As I noticed these hidden gems that I missed when walking in the direction I always go, it struck me that I have been stuck in the way I view life. I had expectations, stubborn ideas, and a one-sided view of the situations happening around me. I wasn't looking for a new, different, fresh way. I was looking at my way.

Your whispered call to change direction resonated with me. My spirit, eyes, and heart needed a new perspective. Yours. In worrying and needing to control the things swirling around me and those I hold dear, I missed Your voice asking me to let go. You see from all directions, all at once, and always will. You have everything sorted and everyone tenderly cared for as Your plans play out in the tapestries You never cease weaving and the prophesies You never cease speaking.

It is surprising what one can see from a different direction and change in perspective. A change of scenery makes such a difference to a weary and stubborn soul. Down every path He takes us, there is always a place to stop, rest a while, and change direction.

The Park Bench
and the Willow Tree

GENTLE SUNBEAMS peek through the branches and leaves of the willow tree. Soft light covers one edge of the wooden park bench beneath its branches.

The sun hasn't been up for very long. The spring morning is quiet and cool after a clear and chilly night. The newly budding leaves are vibrant and proud. They take their job seriously as the givers of shade to the bench and those who visit it.

They are a pair, these two, often referred to as the "willow bench" by those who find solace in the shade and peace from the view of the park. The things the willow bench have seen and heard in their years together—laughter and tears, joy and pain, love, and heartbreak. Anxiety and fear lifted and soothed as the Creator's breath blew healing in the breeze rustling the leaves and cooling the bench-sitter.

His whispered healing is found in bird song, critter antics, fellow bench sitters, and the peace and quiet where words are not needed, where love flows and tenderly holds the wounds poured out in the freedom found under the sweeping branches.

The willow and the park bench have watched seasons come and go. Spring, with the burst of new growth and gentle light from the sun encourages park visitors to venture out and soak up the warmth.

The coming of Summer invites families, picnics, and summer games of baseball, frisbee throwing, and kite flying with the bench and the willow providing shade and rest.

In the Fall, the leaf-peepers and lovers of the season, with their hoodies and warm drinks in hand walk the park. They are filled with anticipation of the changing colors and that feeling of slowing down, coziness, and letting go that Fall always conjures.

There are fewer visitors in Winter when the cold descends. Glimpses of the sun are few and far between. The park folds in on itself as the work of deep rest and hidden growth takes place.

Then there are the faithful ones. Those who visit the bench and the willow no matter the season. They have experienced peace and deep rest here. The wooden bench and gnarled willow are old friends who know their secrets and the pining of the heart and embrace it without words. These park-goers have felt the divine whispers and heavenly songs breathed out over them while sitting in nature's silence. In the shelter and safety of the park bench and the willow tree, they allowed the healing and supernatural presence of the Creator to bind up wounds and lift heavy burdens. With ears that hear and eyes that see, what is sought can be found in the most ordinary and beautiful places.

Summer Night

THE HEAT OF THE DAY is waning. A light breeze picks up in the late afternoon; its drowsy fingers shushing and weaving through the grasses, trees, and flowers. To the West, the sun begins its descent. It defiantly streaks and stains the blue sky with bright oranges and hues of pink as it gives way to the rising half-moon.

One can feel nature's slow sigh as it releases the energy of day into the quiet mystery of night. Birds make one last flight through the garden, snipping up gnats and other nighttime insects. They alight on the bird baths for their last bath and sip of the evening before heading to their nests to cozy down. Safe and snug they await dawn to begin again their songs, flights, and feeding.

As the moon rises higher in the darkening sky it is joined by planets and pinprick stars. Some are still quite faint as they wait their turn to burn bright in the night sky when the sun's afterglow is finished.

As darkness deepens, night-dwellers emerge and begin rustling and creeping through the bushes and grasses as their time to rise and go about their business has arrived. In the cover of darkness all may seem still and at rest, but it's not. The business of nighttime is full, robust, and busy. Tiny garden mice gather and feast on the seeds the raucous birds have scattered in their feeding throughout the day. Their nests are deep underneath the stately ferns and spreading Catmint, giving them excellent cover from the neighborhood cats that hunt and prowl. The cats are part of the night hunters as they stealthily slip between the Lavender, Gaura, and Sage, spying and waiting for an unsuspecting meal.

Fully dark now, the symphony of crickets begins in earnest. It starts with one lone, chirping buzz and is joined by others who've been waiting for nightfall to begin their serenade. The crickets are soon accompanied by the tree frogs that inhabit the nearby marshy open space. It becomes a stage for their croaking and singing. The songs are repetitive and peaceful, allowing the mind to disengage and just be.

Sailing above in a carpet of stars, planets, and zig-zagging satellites, the half-moon is bright, cold, and austere. The simplicity of the light and the cold shine of the moonglow quiets and soothes, gentling away the worries and stress of the day. Deep and peaceful.

Nighttime brings with it a sense of mystery and supernatural portent. Sight cannot be relied upon in the dark. Other senses move to the forefront and must decipher the unseen sounds and goings-on of the night. Discernment is heightened—the soul is what sees and hears.

You are there in the nighttime rustle of the tall grasses as You whisper in the breeze—rest and peace are near. You cause the stars to sing their cold melodies as they shine down. The puzzle pieces of their scattering give direction to the traveler and hope for the lost. Your breath is in the rustling, swooping feathers, and haunting sound of the owl's call as it glides unseen through the dark, cool night. You are always near, the Maestro conducting and guiding all of creation in the symphony of life. There is nowhere I can go where You are not.

Your masterpiece of creation in the still yet busy nighttime is just as lovely, complex, and healing as in the light of day. There is deep healing, peace, and safety in the dark. It requires us to see and hear with our souls and follow Your whispers and songs as You call us into Your marvelous Light.

Go Gently

"LET YOUR GENTLENESS be evident to all. The Lord is near." Philippians 4:5 (NIV)

Go gently into the world today; gentle with yourself and gentle with others.

Go gently as your day unfolds; watch and see who He places in your path.

Go gently letting Kindness guide you, as He opens doors of opportunity to react with softness and tenderness in a world that is suffering, harsh, and rough.

Go gently letting Goodness be your guide, as you bump against those facing pain, loss, and trials beyond your understanding.

Go gently letting Peace direct your steps, as you navigate a world full of anger, hurt, and division.

Go gently letting Joy take you on a journey of delightful surprises, unexpected beauty, and infectious hope that spills and washes over those you encounter.

Go gently letting Love permeate your words and actions as you interact with another who is greatly and extravagantly loved by the Father.

Go gently letting Patience fill you up as you pray for endurance and perseverance for the one struggling to keep up, fearing they will never be enough.

Go gently letting Self-Control infuse you with strength and discernment as temptations and distractions attempt to pierce and blindside as the enemy slithers and prowls.

Go gently letting Faithfulness and devotion keep you in tune with the heart of the Father as you sit at His feet, quench your thirst with life-giving water, and feast at His banqueting table.

Go gently; the Lord is near.

"But the fruit of the Spirit is love, joy, peace, forbearance, kindness, goodness, faithfulness, gentleness, and self-control. Against such things there is no law." Galatians 5:22-23 (NIV)

Presence

Backroads and Quiet Places

MAYBE it's something we do as we grow older or perhaps it's just me. In this second half of my life there's an urgency, not full of panic and fear, but a thrumming in my mind, spirit, and body to make a wide-open space for peace.

Things that once consumed my thoughts and to-do lists fall by the wayside taking a back seat to peace. Fast-paced, non-stop action doesn't hold the same attraction it once did. When I think about how I want to spend my time, my thoughts drift to backroads and quiet places. Peace and His presence.

Opportunities to experience the quiet of a backroads hike, a cabin in the forest, a day at the beach, or sitting around a campfire—this brings me joy. I want to saturate myself with peace in those backroads and quiet places. To be a "good" tired at the end of a day well spent—this is what I crave.

It is easy for busyness to become an idol as we attempt to drown out the shouting, lonely place in our souls with noise and shallow experiences. We don't like to sit with those exposed places in our hearts that are wounded, bleeding, and chaotic. Yet, I think deep down we long for a gentleness to cover, quiet, and soothe, for the chaos to calm and the hurt to be healed. Jesus sees those lonely, messy, hidden places and waits patiently for permission to cleanse and heal all the places that hurt. As He peels back the filthy, ragged, seeping bandages covering the wounds we try so hard to hide, He fills those places with Himself. He is a balm of hope and a safe place for our tired hearts to land. He is a river of joy that washes and cleanses us of the detritus and debris of living life.

So, let's lay at His feet those things that steal life, joy, gratitude, and peace. Let's remember that we are wrapped up in heavenly wings, songs, and delight. We are invited to rest as He opens up the backroads and quiet places that He sprinkles and seasons with His peace.

"He brought me out into a spacious place; he rescued me because he delighted in me." Psalm 18:19 (NIV)

What If...

We are taught not to dwell on the what-ifs. That thought pattern gets a bad rap and we have likely allowed it a place in our mind at some point in our lives. We use the what-if mentality to berate ourselves, dredge up old wounds, and rehash unhappy parts of our past. Giving space to a negative, what-if mentality allows a foothold for regret and bitterness to wedge its way in. These joy-stealers linger and wait in the wings to rob and wither our confidence. What might happen if we turn those what-if statements into encouraging motivators and allow ourselves to step out and be a little risky? Is life truly meant to be lived in a safe and predictable bubble?

Instead of allowing fear to taint our hopes and dreams by listing all the reasons why we could never do it, or someone else could do it better, perhaps we change the narrative.

When we embrace the divine prophecy spoken over us, the what-ifs become a beautiful vision of opportunity to live in harmony with Jesus. Walking with the Divine trailblazer—living in the moment and resting in His safety.

What if we *can* do it and are wildly successful? What if we step out in faith, holding tight to His hand, and simply try? What if the fulfillment we feel brings healing and joy—what if it heals someone else? The sacred intersections and divine appointments experienced as we bump against other sojourners are deliberate and supernatural. All is orchestrated and timed to perfection. His will and our dreams move, breathe, and brush up against those who need what He has entrusted to us and vice versa.

What if we look back on our lives, and instead of regretting that we never tried and lived in fear, we felt covered in freedom and joy? As we live in the purposes and dreams given to us, ripples of love and peace will trail behind us, bringing joy, blessings, and hope to those in their wake.

"Trust in the Lord with all your heart and lean not on your own understanding; in all your ways submit to him and he will make your paths straight."[6]

---

6   Proverbs 3:5-6 NIV

Helpers

I AM A HELPER. It is in my nature to help, fix, and try to make other people's lives easier. I overstep and take on things that are not mine to hold. As an empath, I deeply feel others' joy, sadness, and all the in-between. That's a good thing, right?

Perhaps, but it also gets very heavy. It chokes out my own joy and peace. The burdens of the world are impossible for me to shoulder and quickly take my focus off of being grateful and content. I miss blessings and good things happening in my own life because I feel such a need to help others. I am not equipped to walk another person's path, just as they are not equipped to walk mine.

Matthew 28:18 (NIV) says, "Then Jesus came to them and said, 'All authority in heaven and on earth has been given to me.'"

All authority. All of it. Jesus has the power to rescue, heal, and save. Jesus has the power to change the trajectory of a situation, be miraculous, and guide others along the challenging road ahead of them. There are lessons and truths they alone must walk through and learn. He has that authority. Not me. He is the one weaving our life tapestries.

As I read the above verse in Matthew, I realize that my attempts to fix and make way for another could be rooted in unbelief and that insidious, sneaky need to control, both of which are life and energy thieves. Fear of losing control of how certain things play out in my life and the lives of my loved ones is terrifying to me. I hold on with a white-knuckled grip, trying to manipulate and maneuver circumstances and situations beyond my ability to rehearse and second guess. There are some things that I cannot predict and plan. This is where trust must be allowed to speak and take root. Do I trust Him with those I love? Do I trust Him with me?

In 1 Thessalonians 5:17 (NIV), the apostle Paul exhorts us to "pray continually." How much better would it be for me to use my time and energy to be a good listener, have compassion, pray, help where I am able, and leave the burden and outcome in His omnipotent hands? By praying for someone and asking God to make a way for them, heal them, and love them through me, do I not become a channel of His peace, comfort, and love?

I don't know about you, but this speaks volumes to the helper in me. I sense His gentle breath soothe my heart and pry open my tightly gripped hands. "Let them go. Lay their burdens down. They are safe with Me."

"Whoever dwells in the shelter of the Most High will rest in the shadow of the Almighty. I will say of the Lord, 'He is my refuge and my fortress, my God, in whom I trust'." Psalm 91:1-2 (NIV)

Singing Heart

OPEN space and room to breathe.

It's calling out, and my heart hears it—craving, simmering, and stirring.

A quiet place that will nurture, cradle, and hum the songs of nature, the songs of peace.

A lovely, forest-y meadow path. Beautiful. Full of adventure.

It takes a moment to shed the world as my feet take those first steps.

Social media vies for my attention, hovering in the background. Did that recent post get likes or shares? A snarky comment or minimizing remarks?

"Breathe," whispers the spritely breeze.

"Look," sing the serene trees.

"Just let it go," shout the bright meadow flowers.

Squirrels and fussing birds dart and flit about their business. Purpose.

The pine scent that soothes and calms permeates the slightly chilled air—breathe in and out deeply and fully. Remember.

The silence of the forest and the busyness of the meadow are a beautiful, chaotic contrast—thrilling, healing, and peaceful all at once. Lovely chaos that is joyful, primal, and ancient. Soothing and safe.

Senses are awakened from the hidden place where society often relegates them down to a murmur, a fleeting glimpse, perhaps a burden.

I belong to the elements where senses are welcomed and sights, sounds, scents, and textures are pure. I could be part meadow fairy or tree sprite…

This coming home lifts my spirits as the tight-fisted clenching of muscles, mind, and identity loosens and falls away.

The healing found in nature, the elements, and life in the quiet places is spiritual, miraculous, and mysterious.

Divine whispers surround, swirl, and permeate the soul, spirit, and heart, bringing pure delight, unfettered joy, and hope.

As I drink it in, scraping off the expectations, demands, and "shoulds" that cling to my heart, I feel a melody pumping through my veins.

A release and crescendo beating in time to the songs of nature and the quiet places lovingly woven by the Creator.

Healing, belonging, and peace flood in to fuel the song and seal in my mind's eye and heart-memory, the wonder and serenity of this less traveled road to peace.

My heart sings to the rhythms of Creation.

The Lord Establishes...

"IN THEIR HEARTS humans plan their course, but the Lord establishes their steps." Proverbs 16:9 (NIV)

Simmer in that for a minute. Allow the words to wash over you. Letting God establish our steps...

If you are a planner, a list-maker, or a white knuckle, vise-grip controller, these simple words bump against the ordered and safe world we are trying to create for ourselves. Our lists and plans give us the illusion of control and predictability in a world that increasingly feels anything but safe. Lists and plans feel tucked in and protected. The idea of giving Jesus the wheel feels frightening and chaotic—a free fall into no-man's land. The not knowing and the inability to rehearse and prepare is terrifying.

But...What if not knowing holds incredible beauty and life-changing adventures? He declared His purpose and plans over us as He sang us into existence in the presence of cherubim and angels. He knows our comings and goings, our thoughts, and fears. Perhaps letting go and walking the path He's established for us will usher in peace, protection, excitement, and rest. Isn't that what we are seeking?

He knows our past, present, and future as it intertwines and connects us to the Divine order already in place. It is wild, fierce, and untamed by the frailty of human attempts at planning and controlling. It is contradictory and mysterious, this calm in the chaos, this order in the untamed. Yet we are asked to trust Him with us—to hold tightly to His hand and just be. Do we trust Him?

Clenched fists can relax, and stiff necks can swivel as we breathe, hold hands with the Divine, and take in the blessings and thrills He sprinkles along our journey. God setting the pace. God establishing our steps. There is a pace and rhythm—it is Divine, and it is perfect.

There will be bumps, valleys, and sometimes chasms to navigate, but He knows where they are. He walks ahead as our Light, walks with us as our Friend, and stands behind us as our rear guard. We will be helped over, around, and through whatever is before us as His staff removes obstacles and banishes our enemies. We have nothing to fear. God is for us, and nothing can stand against us.

Isaiah 41:10 (NIV): "So do not fear, for I am with you; do not be dismayed, for I am your God. I will strengthen you and I will help you; I will uphold you with my righteous right hand."

He is Near

Psalm 139:7-10 (NIV): "Where can I go from your Spirit? Where can I flee from your presence? If I go up to the heavens, you are there; if I make my bed in the depths, you are there. If I rise on the wings of the dawn, if I settle on the far side of the sea, even there your hand will guide me, your right hand will hold me fast."

While the moon begins its descent giving way to the dawn, the Lord is near.

As the last vestiges of nighttime dreams drift away, the Lord is near.

In the early morning, as the sun rises to bathe the world in light, the Lord is near.

As you stretch and greet a new day filled with untold adventure, the Lord is near.

When your morning coffee brings warmth to your hands and a smile to your face, the Lord is near.

In the garden as you tend to the flowers and prune off the withered and dying places, the Lord is near.

Dozing in the hammock under the purple Lilac tree, the Lord is near.

As the honeybees peacefully drone and buzz about the bright-colored, lovely blooms, the Lord is near.

In line at the coffee shop as you observe humanity come and go, the Lord is near.

When the scared and frail homeless woman watches people pass her by without a glance or an offer to help, the Lord is near.

As you receive a blindsiding diagnosis and panic freezes your heart, the Lord is near.

When despair causes deep pain and loneliness, the Lord is near.

When hurtful words come against you in anger and rejection, the Lord is near.

He is found in a breathtaking sunrise, a raging storm, a kind smile, and deep conversations. He is found in the loud and frenetic just as often as the mundane and unobtrusive, where the chaos of the world and humanity is stilled.

The Lord is near as He listens attentively to your softest utterance and answers your silent need.

He is near when you recognize His voice in compassionate whispers that rustle the leaves and hover over you in the breeze— the mystery of deep calling to deep.

When you seek Him, He will be found. Peace and hope are waiting for you. Listen for His whispers. The Lord is near.

Jeremiah 29:12-14 (NIV): "Then you will call upon me and come and pray to me, and I will listen to you. You will seek me and find me when you seek me with all your heart. I will be found by you," declares the Lord, "and will bring you back from captivity."

Weakness

THE SUN hasn't been up for long. I'm sitting in my favorite spot with my coffee, of course. I am feeling out of sorts and restless this morning. The patio and garden are cool and lovely with early birds and neighborhood critters stopping in for breakfast. I know there is peace to be found here, but it's elusive. Things are weighing on my heart, and circumstances happening that leave me feeling feeble, out of control, and uncertain. These are not feelings I like. I don't want them hanging around making me feel afraid and incapable.

My mind is trying to process and organize all these things—trying to fix them because I fancy myself a fixer. As I'm sitting, a breeze picks up and tosses leaves and spent blooms around the garden. I notice that they are at the mercy of the breeze. It isn't a wild and insane storm; it is simply a breeze that is stronger than the blooms—the blooms are weaker than the breeze. Pondering this, remembered words pop into my mind... *My strength comes into its own in your weakness.*

Weakness. This isn't a word most of us want to ascribe to ourselves. However, strength needs weakness. When we are at the end of ourselves is when Jesus has room to come in with His strength to protect and do the miraculous. I don't believe He views our weakness as something to look down on or shake His head at in annoyance. I believe He views our weakness as a beautiful opportunity to shower us with His grace, love, and protection—to impart His perfect strength into us and our circumstances. He shows us glimpses of the future as He opens and closes doors. We see a foreshadowing of eternity as we watch Him do the impossible, comforting and healing us when life doesn't turn out how we prayed it would.

He is the Weaver of our life tapestry. He sees the beginning, middle, and end. He intimately knows where our lives will intersect with another's journey. Perhaps the unique and specific strengths He has given us will be exactly what is needed to help another—our strength perfectly matched to their circumstances.

Weakness doesn't have to hold a negative connotation. It has much more depth than that. Perhaps there is a richness to it that speaks of humanity needing each other to get through life.

In another's weakness we get the wonderful opportunity to be His hands, feet, and comfort. We are also blessed with opportunities to be on the receiving end of another's strength. The life-song of humanity is a thing of beauty that intersects and strengthens as we witness startling acts of bravery and kindness, a chance to bring hope. There is beauty in weakness.

Clutter

FOR THOSE OF US to-do list lovers who get great satisfaction as we make neat tick marks, cross off, or scribble out each line on the list, it feels like a goal has been met as we watch that list dwindle. Accomplishment, focused, and successful. And it is all of those things—an errand completed, a task finished, control over our day. Control. There's that word again. It seems to be a theme in my life, and maybe it is in yours, too. When I make my lists and check things off I feel like I am controlling, planning, and maintaining my life in a healthy and well-kept way. And for a little while, I am. But, if I examine how my life feels from a different perspective, I notice that many things on my to-do list are not necessarily things that bring me joy or happiness, or give me permission to rest. Yes, I am pleased when my home is clean and organized and when phone calls and emails are returned and handled. It's a good feeling, and those are necessary accomplishments, but at the same time it feels devoid of simple pleasures, of peace.

In an effort to bring peace into my life, I put it on my to-do list and schedule time for myself as a calendar-ed event. There is nothing wrong with this. However, for me, it sometimes falls flat, feeling lackluster and forced. There is a lot of pressure to make that time perfectly peaceful and in the striving and worrying about whether or not I'm feeling peace, it ends up a frustrating and tiring experience.

Philippians 4:6-7 (NIV) says, "Do not be anxious about anything, but in every situation, by prayer and petition, with thanksgiving, present your requests to God. And the peace of God, which transcends all understanding, will guard your hearts and your minds in Christ Jesus."

The peace of God. Not the peace that I force and manufacture for myself or the momentary and fleeting peace I feel when a task is ticked off of that constant and never-ending to-do list. The peace of God. Peace that transcends all understanding, all lists, and the clutter of humanity in this oftentimes chaotic world. The peace of God redefines what a successful and accomplished day might look like if I let go of the idea of an uncluttered day. Finding Him in the midst of the clutter and accepting each day as it comes, perhaps even allowing some things to be undone at the end of the day, could be the very thing that ushers in peace and the simple joys I am seeking.

Anxiety over an unfinished to-do list has the potential to rob you and me of beautiful times of rest and peace just sitting with a cup of coffee, walking leisurely along the beach, reading a book, and talking to Jesus. I don't want my endless lists to become an idol that takes the place of His peace. When my day is peppered with quick prayers, ongoing conversations with Him, and following His lead throughout the day, my definition of success changes.

A successful day can look like napping when our bodies are worn down, giving ourselves a little more time to complete errands and tasks, laughing and sharing with a friend, or listening for His whispers in the wind chimes on the patio. It will look different for all of us, and that is the beauty of Jesus—the One who knows us best. He knows how we need to experience His presence. When we welcome Him in to guide us through our day, the clamor of the clutter dims and fades in the power of His peace. God's peace. It is a guard and shield over our hearts that filters out all that demands our time and robs us of joy. He gives us permission to lavishly rest and bask in His life-giving peace. Restoration. Healing. Peace.

Simple Treasures

BEFORE YOU OPEN your eyes to welcome a new day, the Father has each moment planned out in perfect detail. This new day was prepared with tender care and concern, no detail left loose or unfinished. Perfection. Purpose.

The warmth of the rising sun peeping through the bedroom window leaves streaks and ribbons of light, waking you from a night of slumber and dreams. The soft purrs from sleepy kitties in the path of these light ribbons feel homey and comforting. Content. Safe.

The aroma of brewing coffee and the scent of spring waft pleasantly on the breeze floating through the kitchen window. It refreshes and perks up the senses. Alive and well.

Birdsong in the busy garden soothes and speaks to the still-waking mind. All carefully orchestrated, all for you. Peace.

The delight of finding new growth in the budding spring flowers infuses you with joy and excitement as you putter and fuss in the garden. He delights in hiding well-placed surprises to bring a smile to your face. You are the apple of His eye. Beloved.

The three-tiered fountain sings and chatters as rays of sunlight create dazzling rainbows in the splashing water. It's such a joyful, bubbling, and carefree sound! Energy and happiness fill your heart as you listen to the random pattern of the cascading water. Invigorating!

Returning home after a busy morning of errands, you slip off your shoes and head outside with a book, iced tea, and a bowl of mixed nuts. Situating yourself on a hammock under the apple tree, the beauty and peace of the quiet afternoon flow around you. Yellow and black bumblebees buzz and drowse among the newly opened flowers. Next to the stone birdbath, colorfully delicate butterflies flit around the fragrant purple blossoms of the Butterfly bush. Hummingbirds sip the Honeysuckle and hover over the bright pink Freesia flowers. You feel loved, safe, and blissful. A beautiful afternoon designed just for you. Rest.

Evening falls, and the air grows chilly. Heading inside you begin winding down for the night. With a cup of hot green tea in your hand, you reflect on all that happened during this day. The snippets and bits of joy and peace you discovered wrap you up like the fleecy blanket thrown over your legs. The sleepy white cat kneads and purrs on your lap, then settles in for a snooze. Your Father knew what you needed today as He walked with you in peaceful places and shielded you from things not meant for you. His Presence ministered peace to your heart, soul, and spirit. Abundance and blessings. You are deeply loved and cherished.

Psalm 34:8 (NIV): "Taste and see that the Lord is good; blessed is the one who takes refuge in him."

Every Good and Perfect Gift

THE DAY is winding down. Putting on the tea kettle, I stand at the kitchen sink, looking over the garden in the slowly dimming light. There are still birds and plump squirrels investigating the bird feeders and taking their evening baths before the sun fully sets. The frogs in the marshy area of the open space begin their evening chorus. Their song is soothing, and I look forward to this acapella performance each evening as a gift from nature that I get to unwrap.

The shouting kettle calls that it's teatime, so I pour hot, steamy water into my mug with the word Serenity written in bold, black letters, the aroma of the Portland Blend black tea rising up. My hands are warm from the tea. A feeling of calm settles on my shoulders as my mind wanders back over my day, recounting what transpired and all the blessings…

As usual, the dog and cats woke me up early, insistent that the established routine be followed. They don't forget, so it's best to get up and start the day—besides, coffee will be waiting! Their dependence on me for all their needs touches me. These beautiful creatures love and need me. It is wonderful to be needed and trusted. The gifts of joy and unconditional love they offer in return are invaluable.

A morning spent volunteering with like-minded people who have a heart for those needing extra help feeding their families brings me joy. I'm tired at the end of the shift, but it's a good tired. Helping take some of the worry and fear off of the shoulders of a weary mom, a struggling dad, and a tired grandma is humbling. It's a beautiful gift.

Afternoon chats with moms of soldiers who have similar fears and worries as our sons serve and protect our country are something I never take for granted. They understand it all. The support we give and receive is a beautiful and treasured gift. Heartfelt conversations with dear friends, their prayers, and the safety to share the good and not-so-good are gifts that I don't take lightly. Blessings wrapped up as beautiful humans. Treasures.

As I ponder the events of my day, I realize there were many small but not insignificant gifts that God showered on me, things that might go unnoticed but made a positive difference. Such as a good parking place, cheerful birdsong, sunlight filtering through the clouds, a compliment from a stranger, and giving and receiving kindness and words of encouragement.

By intentionally seeking out the gifts placed in our lives, our perspective changes from one of anxious worry to hopeful anticipation of the lovely gifts we can unwrap as each day unfolds.

There is joy in simply thinking about the intentionality and love our Father has for us. It is hard to grasp that I am so loved and cherished that I have His undivided attention. He blends up joy, surprise, laughter, and intricate detail into every day I am blessed to wake up. He is doing this for you, too.

There will be days that are hard to endure, with unwanted things that blindside and wound. That is never to be dismissed or minimized. My limited understanding cannot explain it. But perhaps, in the midst of all the hard and unwanted, the calm and the peaceful, there are deeply personal and breathtaking treasures waiting to be discovered. I believe He delights in placing them in the midst of our messy and chaotic humanity—waiting for us to look around in expectation for the good and the lovely because He is good, lovely, and trustworthy. I love what Psalm 37:3 & 4 (NIV) says, "Trust in the Lord and do good; dwell in the land and enjoy safe pasture. Take delight in the Lord, and he will give you the desires of your heart."

Settling in for the night under my blankets with softly purring cats, I feel calm. Yes, there is still chaos and hard things swirling and poking for a place to seep in and cause worry, but the weight of them is kept at bay, at least for the moment. I turn my attention to the gifts I was blessed with today and allow my mind to wander and wonder at what I might find tomorrow...

James 1:17 (NIV): "Every good and perfect gift is from above, coming down from the Father of the heavenly lights, who does not change like shifting shadows."

Whispers

It's FOUND in the delicate breath of air tousling the hair and swaying the wind chimes. The tinkling music calms and gentles the wound-up heart.

The murmuring splashes of a springtime brook as clear water makes its way through, over, and around little dams, rocks, and detritus soothes and cleanses.

It is heard along the forest trail as the wind sighs through the pine canopy in the late afternoon, signaling the lazy descent of the sun. Peace and rest are on the way.

The gentle hum and thrum of bees busy at work in the lavender and rosemary allow a tired mind to wander and doze on a warm afternoon spent on a garden lounge chair. Calm and serene.

Bird song, as the summer sun rises over the hills, pours joy and cheer into a sleepy body—good things are on the way.

Raindrops on the patio roof offer a restless heart the soothing song of monotony and replenishment as the mind stills and slows. Peaceful.

The crackles and snaps of a merry campfire delight and mesmerize as random bursts and flares of light and fire transfix and drowse after a day of hiking.

Steam rising from hot coffee dances and zips on the whim of the breeze as the Creator speaks, sings, and whispers to His beloved the joy, hope, and sweet promises of Presence. His whispers are all around us.

Author Bio

Melissa Giomi, author of *Divine Encounters...*, *Divine Appointments...*, and *Divine Whispers...* is a Northern California native born in Redding. She lives near San Francisco with her husband and their pets. They have two adult children.

Melissa is passionate about Jesus, nature, writing, and gardening. She enjoys good coffee, mornings spent on the patio, deep connections, and meaningful conversations. Melissa and her husband enjoy trying new restaurants, relaxing by the ocean, hiking, and camping in the Redwoods.

Journeying through life's changing seasons, Melissa discovered that God often speaks in gentle whispers on a soft breeze and in the beauty of nature. All that's needed is a heart ready to receive Him and eyes open to seek Him.